Hi, my name is Sammy

Follow me on the road to Safety →

Do not Litter on the bus

Sammy says littering on the bus is messy so always throw your trash away in the trash container before you get on the bus.

We like to keep the bus clean for the next person that rides the bus.

Litter on the floor can cause accidents so be cool and be clean!

It's important that you sit forward in your seat while you are on the bus because if the driver has to make a sudden stop, you have a better chance of not falling down and getting hurt.

We want you to get home safe so remember to follow the rules.

Do not eat, drink or chew gum on the bus

Please don't eat, drink or chew gum on the bus. There are many reasons this can be unsafe.

If someone starts choking, the driver may not see that person choking. The driver may be busy driving.

Also, it's not very polite to eat in front of others. So, please keep any food or drinks at the school, at home or safely tucked away in your backpack.

Be nice
No bad words

Please be nice to each other and don't say any bad words. Sometimes the words can hurt someone's feelings.

If you are angry at someone then don't speak to them. Talk to the driver or your teacher so they can help you solve any problems.

That's the smart way! Stay cool!

No animals on the bus

Unfortunately, we cannot allow animals or insects on the bus.

It's too much of a distraction for some of the other riders and may pose a health risk to us humans.

So play it safe and keep them somewhere safe like school or home.

Speak softly
No Yelling

Sammy likes you to speak softly. It's hard to hear an important noise if everyone is talking loud.

If the driver has something important to tell you, you may not be able to hear him or her if it's too loud on the bus.

The driver needs to listen to the dispatcher in case there is important information the driver needs to know, like construction work and blocked roads.

That way, the driver can take a better route and get you home on time.

Obey the Driver

Respect others on the bus

It is very important that you listen carefully to the driver when the driver is talking to you. Why? Because, the driver is responsible for getting you home safe.

The driver has to watch for all kinds of unsafe things on the road. For example, if the driver wants you to be quiet, it may be because he or she is listening for a train or maybe they heard someone else on the bus that needs help.

You should be nice to others on the bus, too. Respect each other. That's the coolest thing you can do.

No throwing objects out of the window

Please don't throw anything out of the school bus windows. You might accidentally hit someone or a car outside of the bus and they could get hurt or it could cause a car crash.

Also, we want to keep the earth nice and clean. So wait until the driver has reached your stop and is ready to let you get up. Then you can throw your trash away in the trash can.

1. Arrive <u>5</u> minutes early to your bus stop.
2. Stand in line.
3. Wait until the bus <u>stops</u> and the door is <u>open</u>.

Please arrive at your stop 5 minutes early. Also, stand in line and DO NOT run up to the bus while it is approaching. That is very dangerous.

So please wait until the bus has stopped and the bus door has opened for you.

We want to remind you that it is not a race to get on the bus. We will always have a seat for you.

Please do not block the aisle

Please do not block the aisle with your legs and/or your belongings.

If there is any emergency, we need the aisle open to get to those who need us. Also, someone may trip over something while getting on or getting off the bus and they could fall and get hurt.

So please sit straight with your legs in front of you and keep your belongings under the seat for safe keeping.

Keep your
Head   Hands

and

Feet

Inside the bus
at all times

Let's be safe and keep our hands, head and feet in the bus at all times.

We don't want you to get hurt for any reason. So, if you want to wave at a friend, you can wave to them from inside the bus.

Remember, safety first!

Stay seated until the bus stops

Stay seated until the bus comes to a complete stop.

If you get up too soon, you might fall down and we won't want you to hurt yourself. Sometimes, unexpected things happen while the driver is trying to pull over and he or she may have to suddenly stop the bus.

So it's much safer for you to stay in your seat.

About the Author

Marianne Kelly lives and works in Northern California. She is a divorced Mom with three active teenagers.

Marianne has been a school bus driver in the San Francisco Bay Area for many years. Her specialty is transporting special needs students.

Art has been a part of Marianne's life since childhood. She credits her Mother, an accomplished artist in her own right, for her artistic talent.

Produced by Norma Brock
Copyright Marianne Kelly 2000
Published by CreateSpace, a DBA of On-Demand Publishing, LLC
amazon.com

Made in the USA
Middletown, DE
06 April 2018